The Commuting Colorist

Travel Size Series - Cars

by Patricia Markham

Travel size coloring books are specially made with the commuting colorist in mind. Great designs are formatted to fit easily into backpacks, flight bags, and briefcases. Take them on the road, in the air, or keep them on hand for lunch and coffee breaks. Make creative use of spare minutes anywhere.

Thank you for purchasing "The Commuting Colorist." If you enjoy this book of designs, please take a moment to give it a 5 star rating on Amazon and leave a positive comment. While you're there (on Amazon) look for other books by Patricia Markham.

Look for other books
by author and illustrator
Patricia Markham

Epiphany Park Publishing
March 2018
All rights reserved

Credit for the original designs in this book goes to the many artists who contribute their fine work to the galleries of pixabay.com.

Test your colors here.
If you are using markers, it is recommended to place a blotter behind the page you are working on in order to perserve the next design.

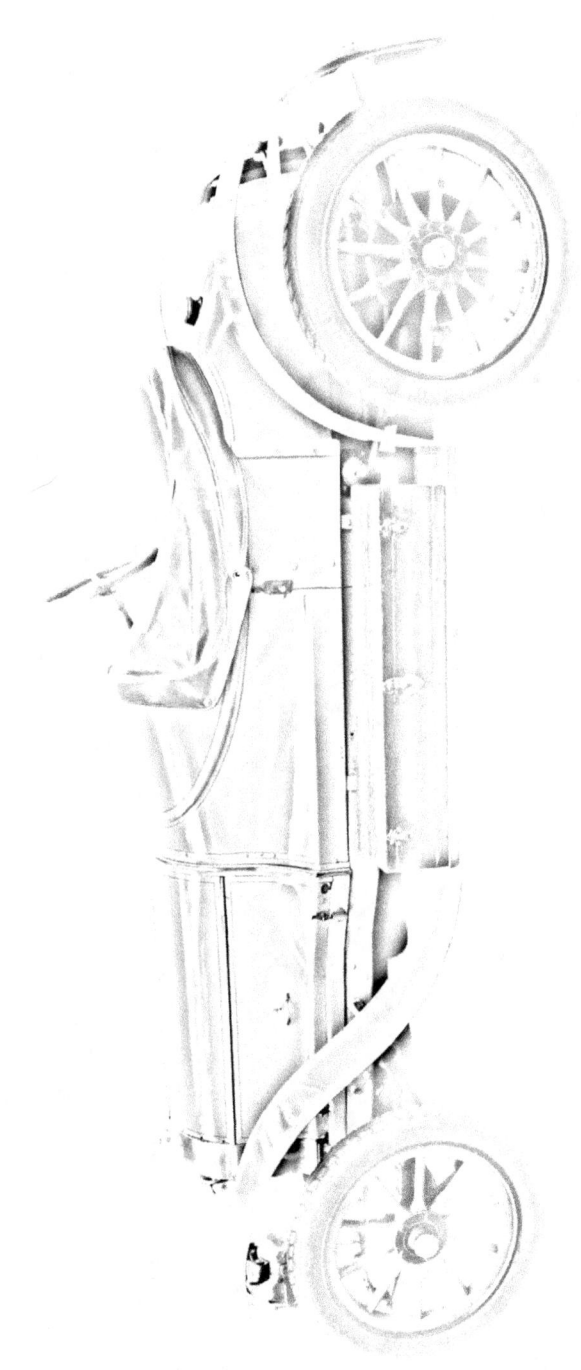

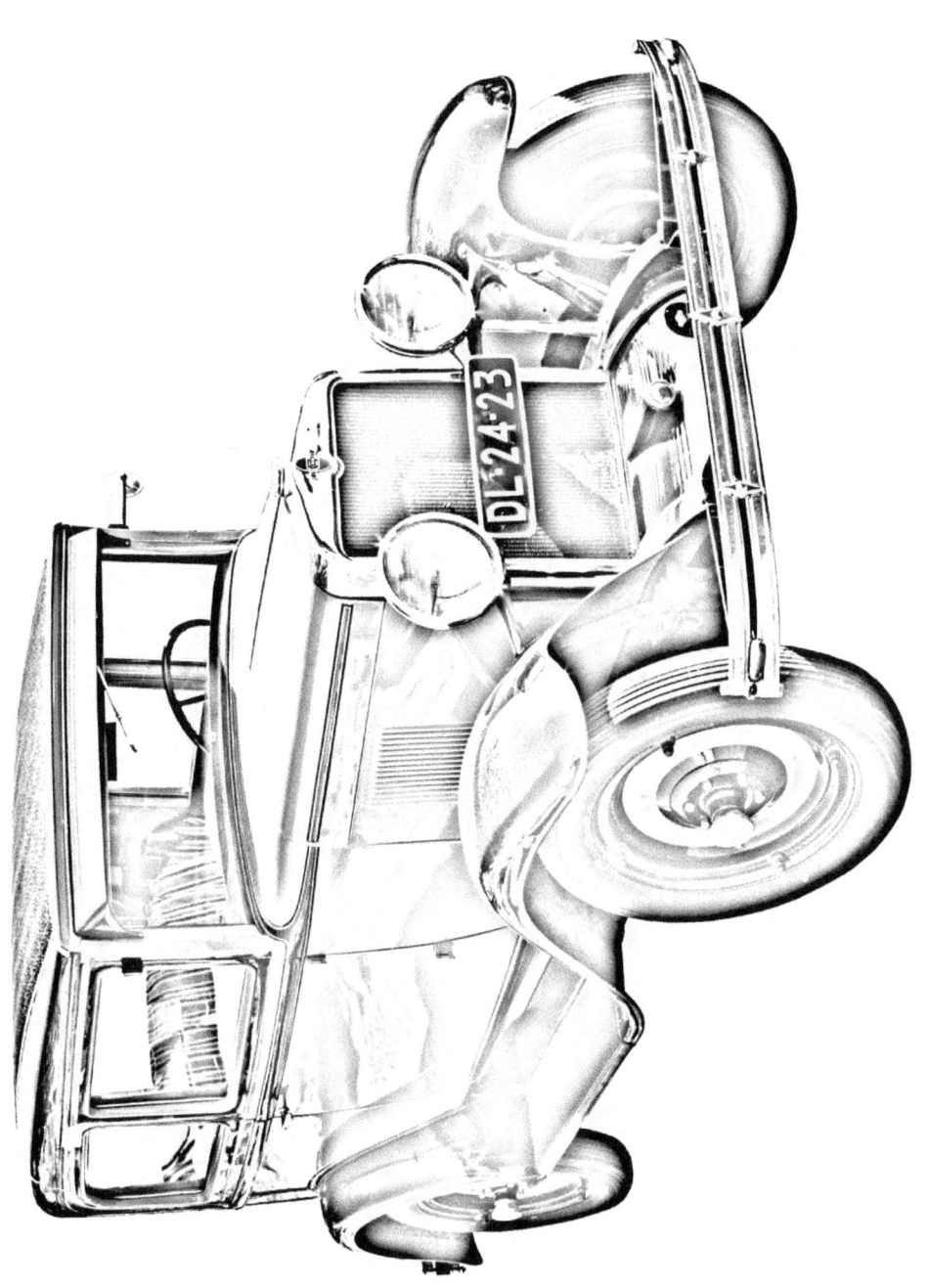

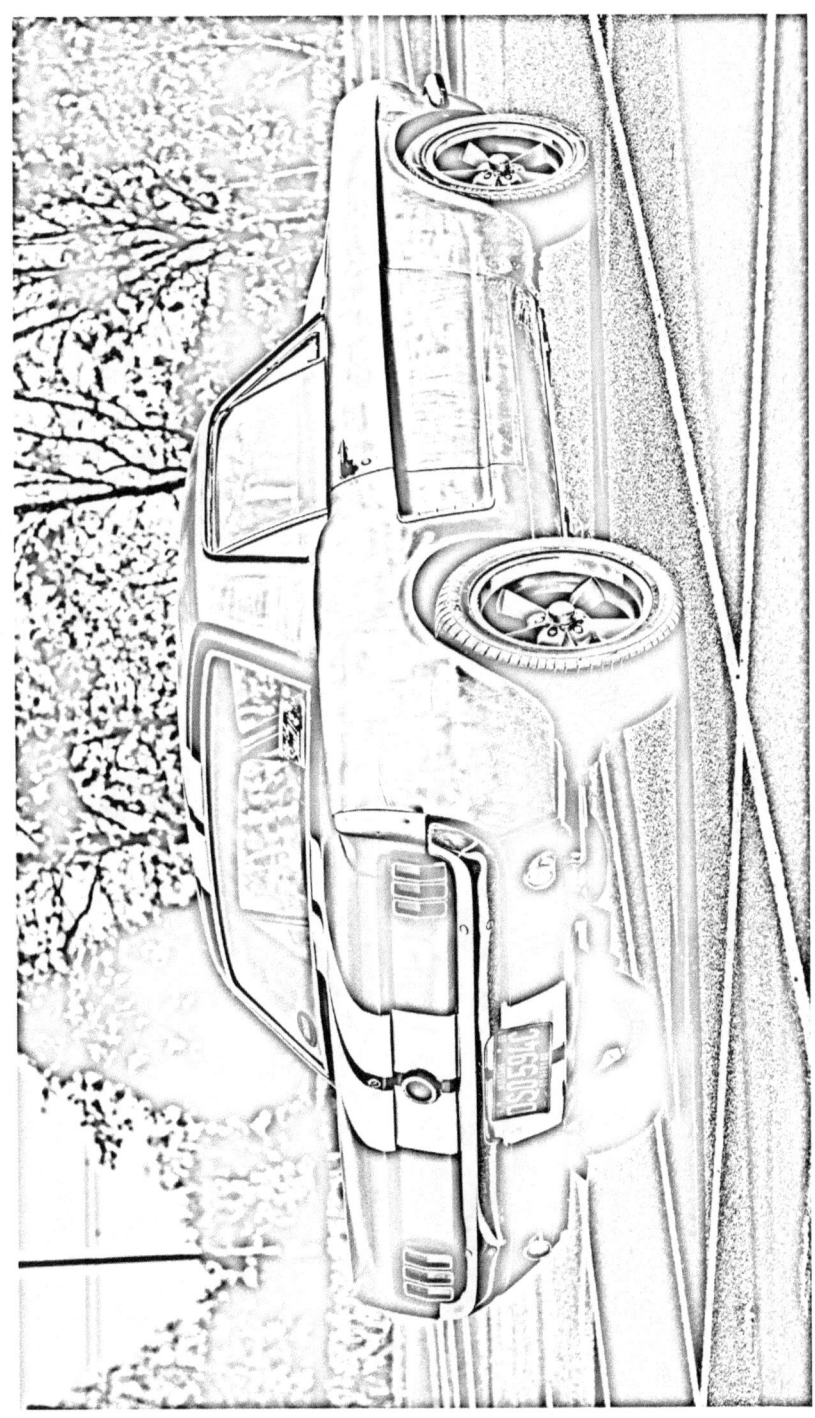

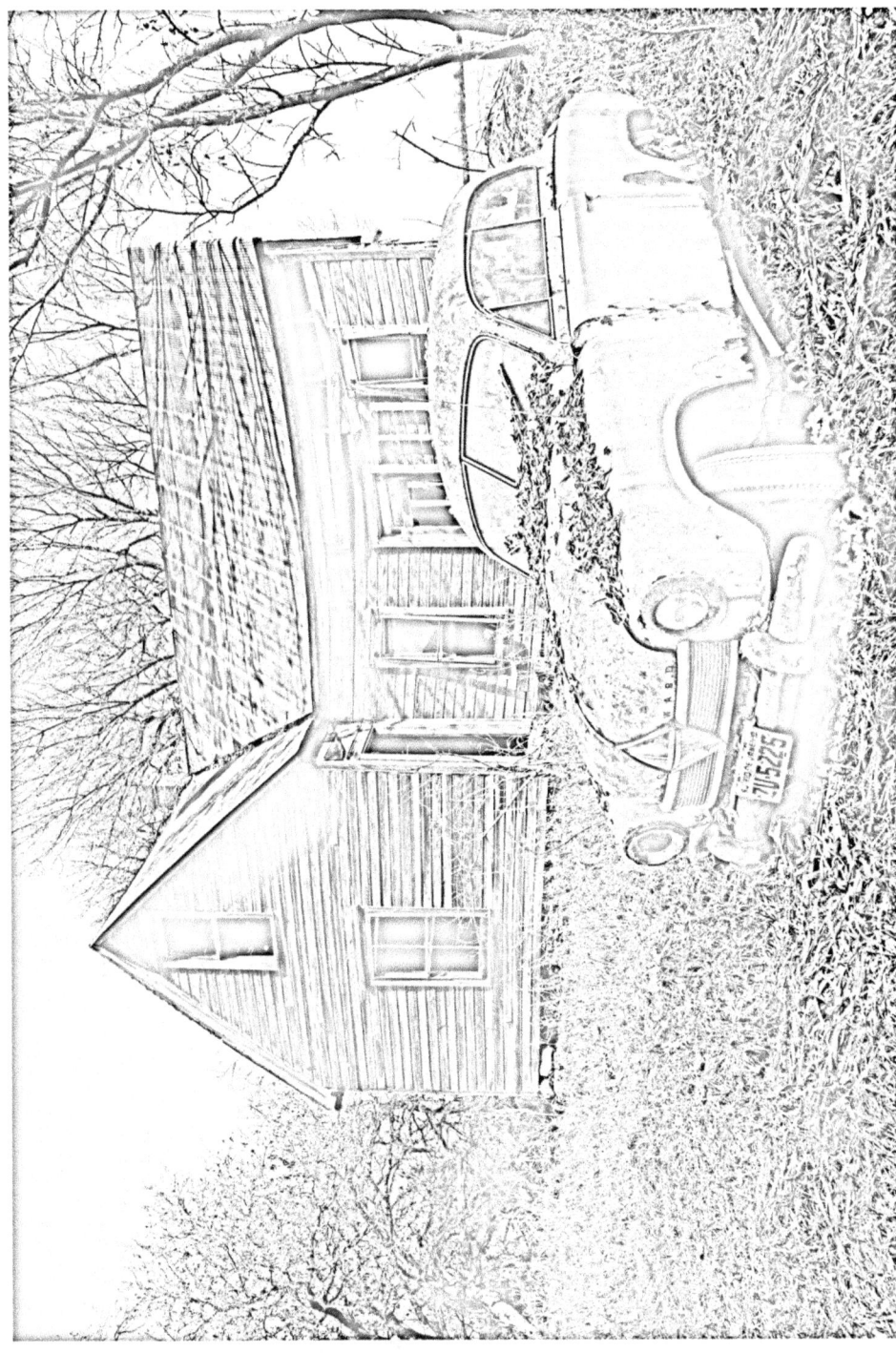

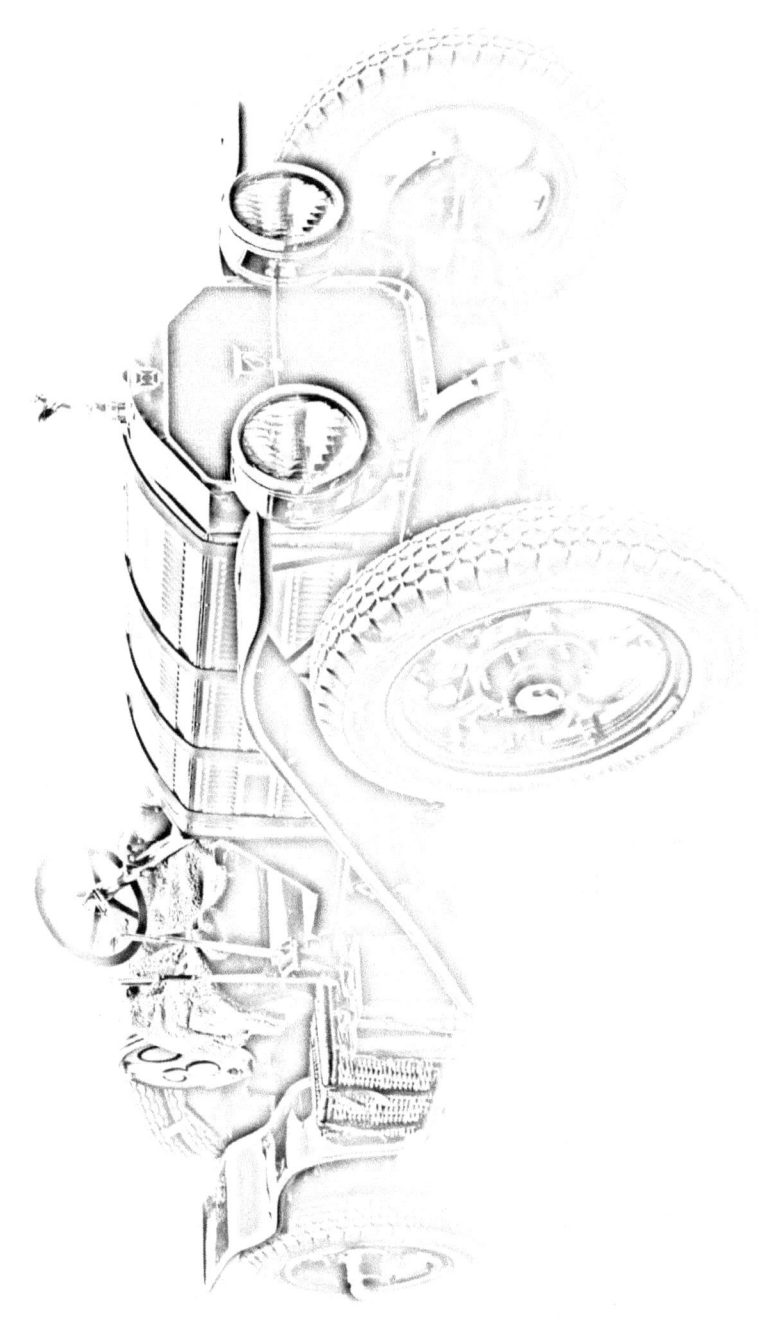

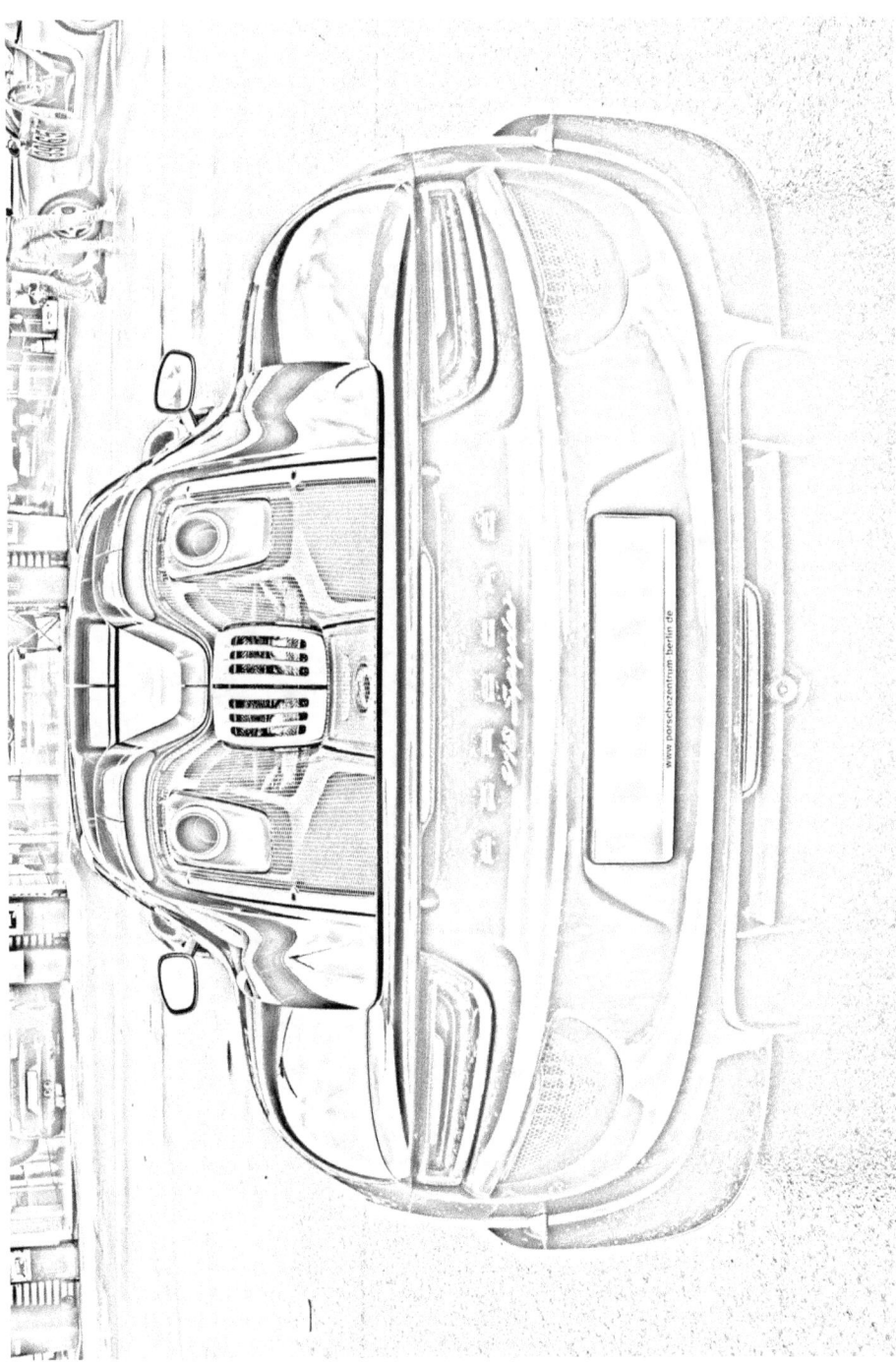

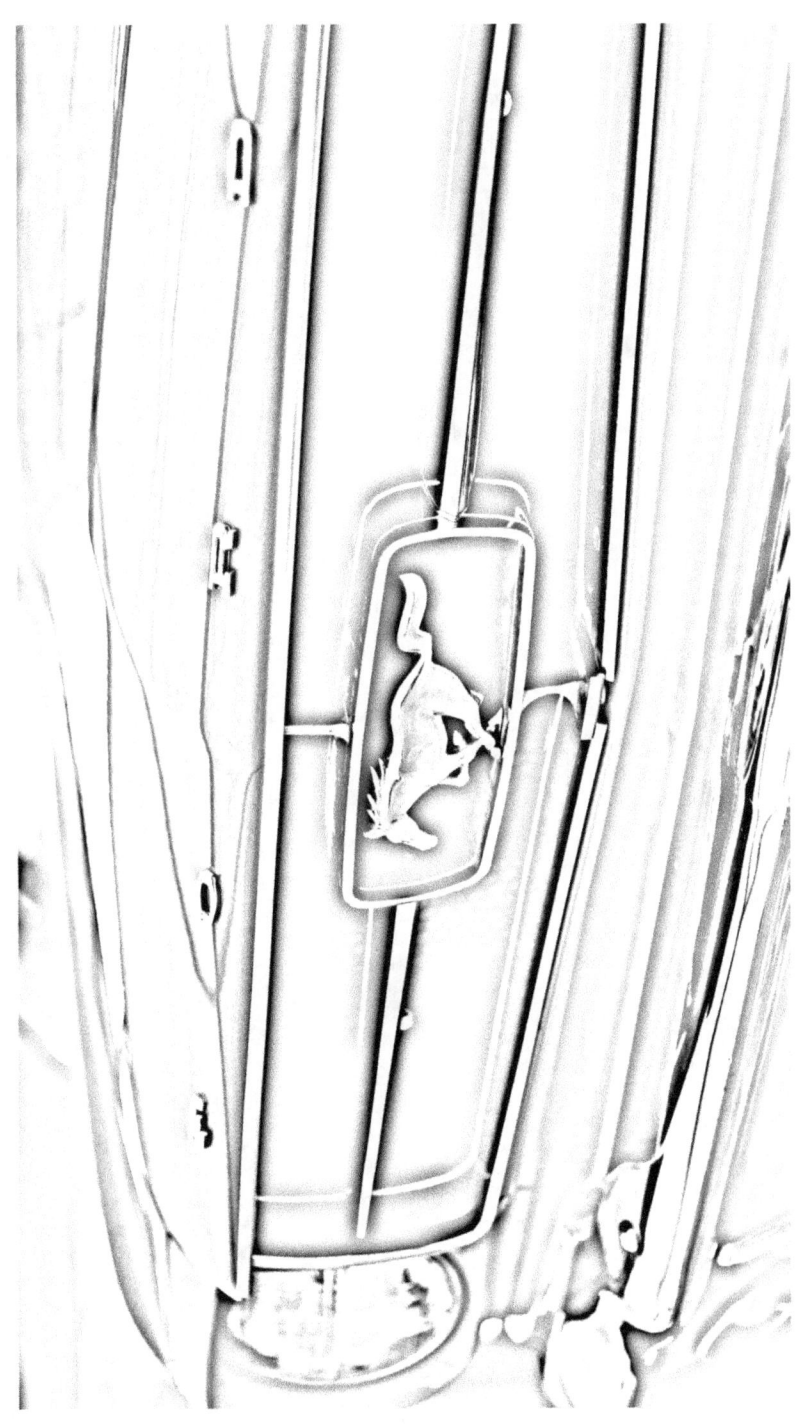

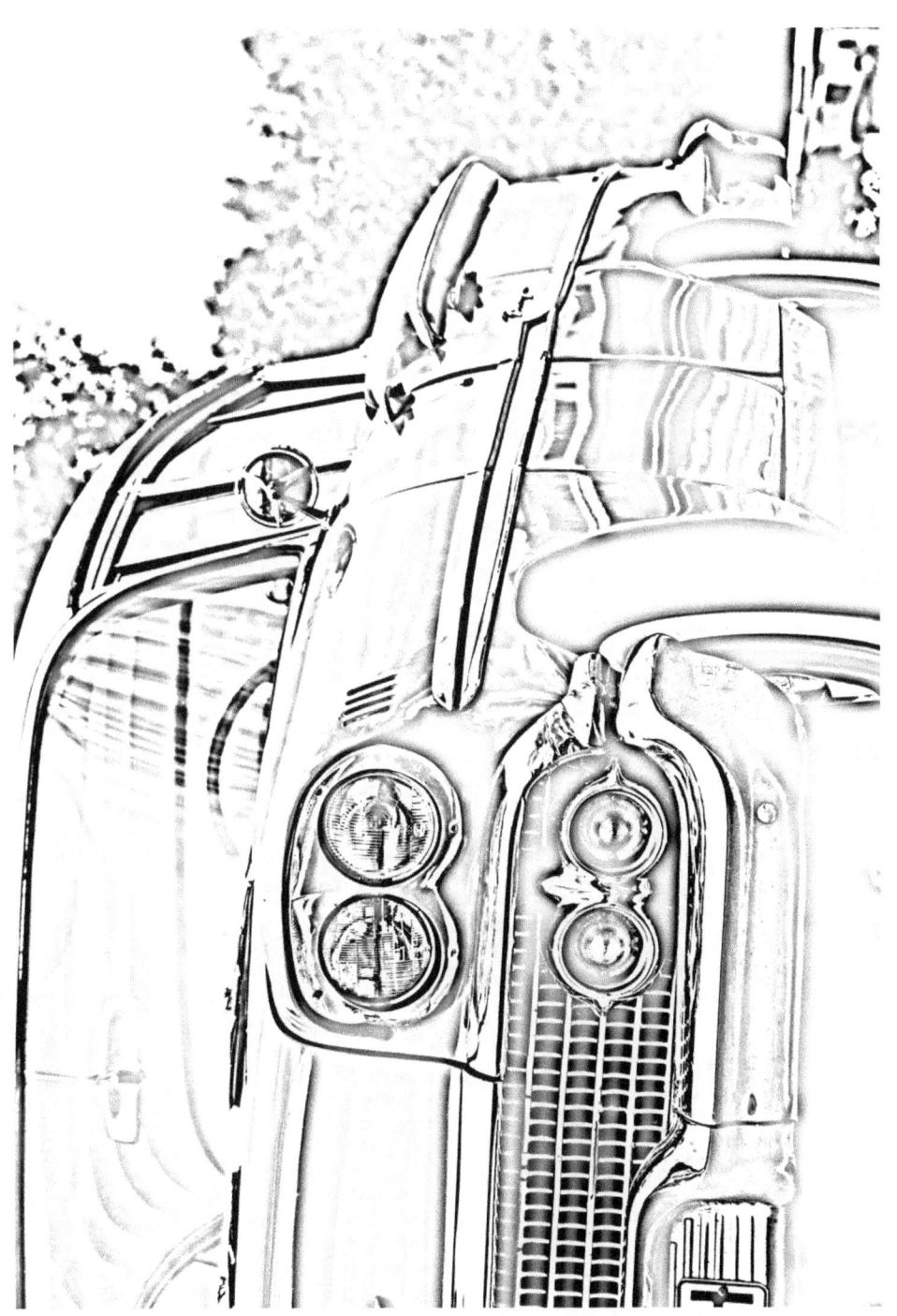

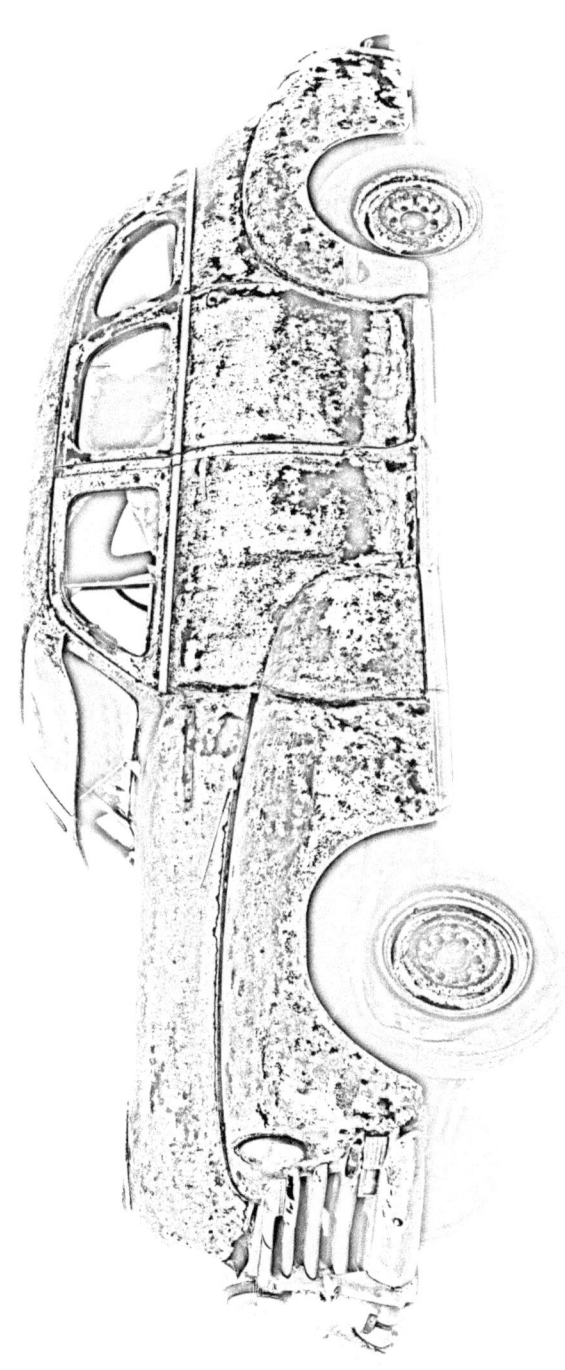

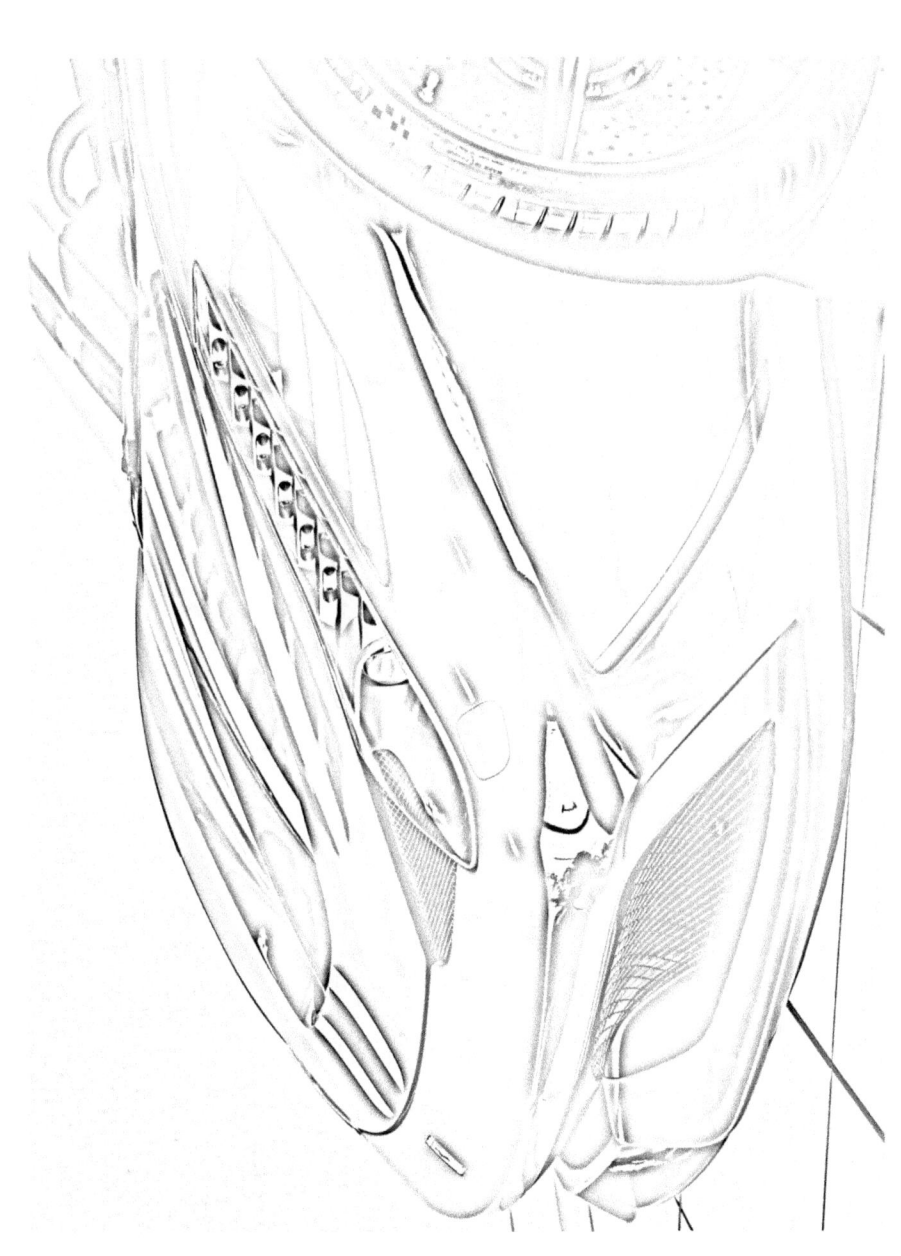

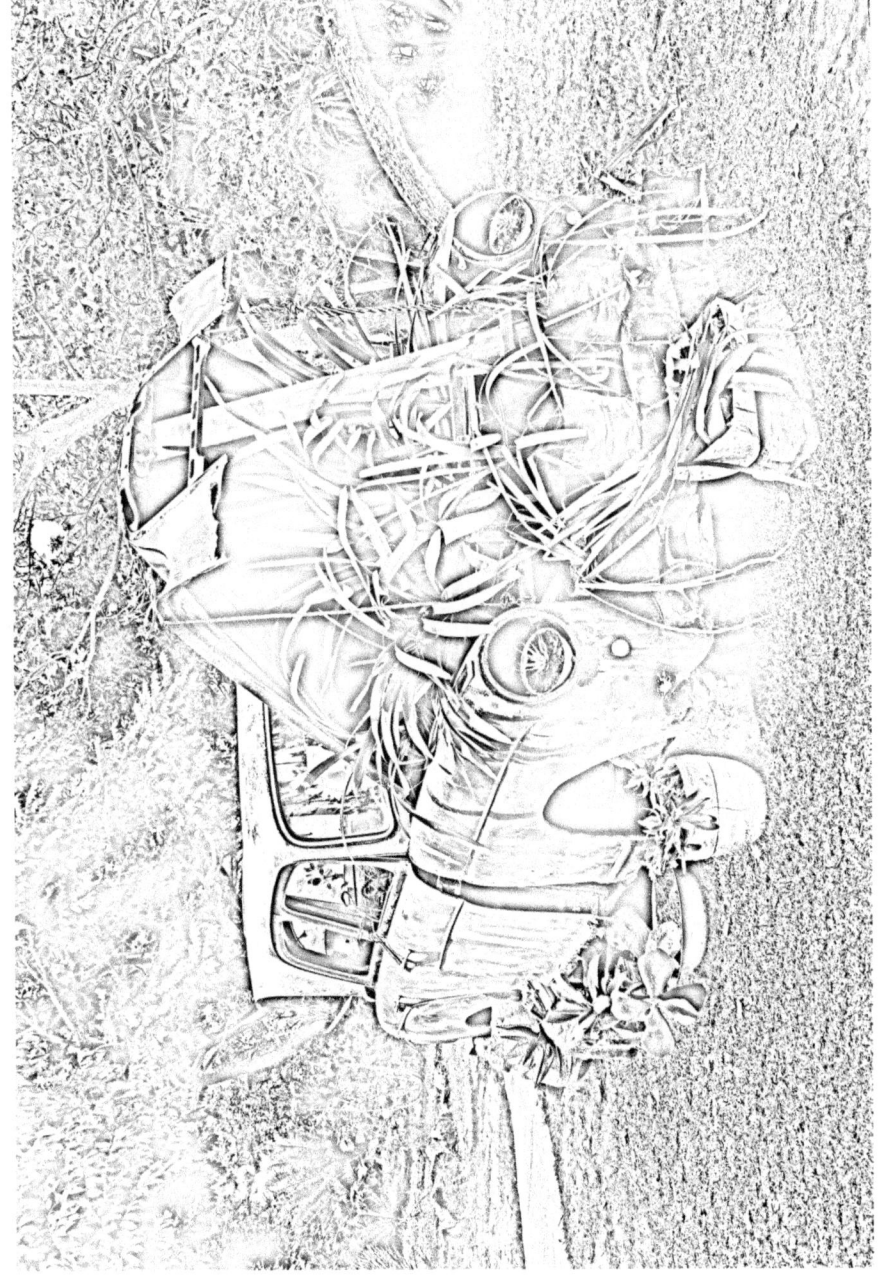

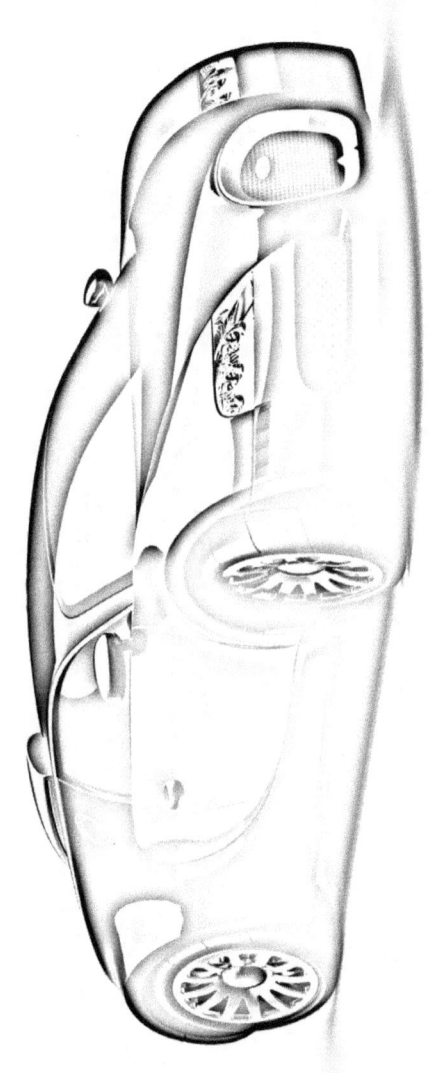

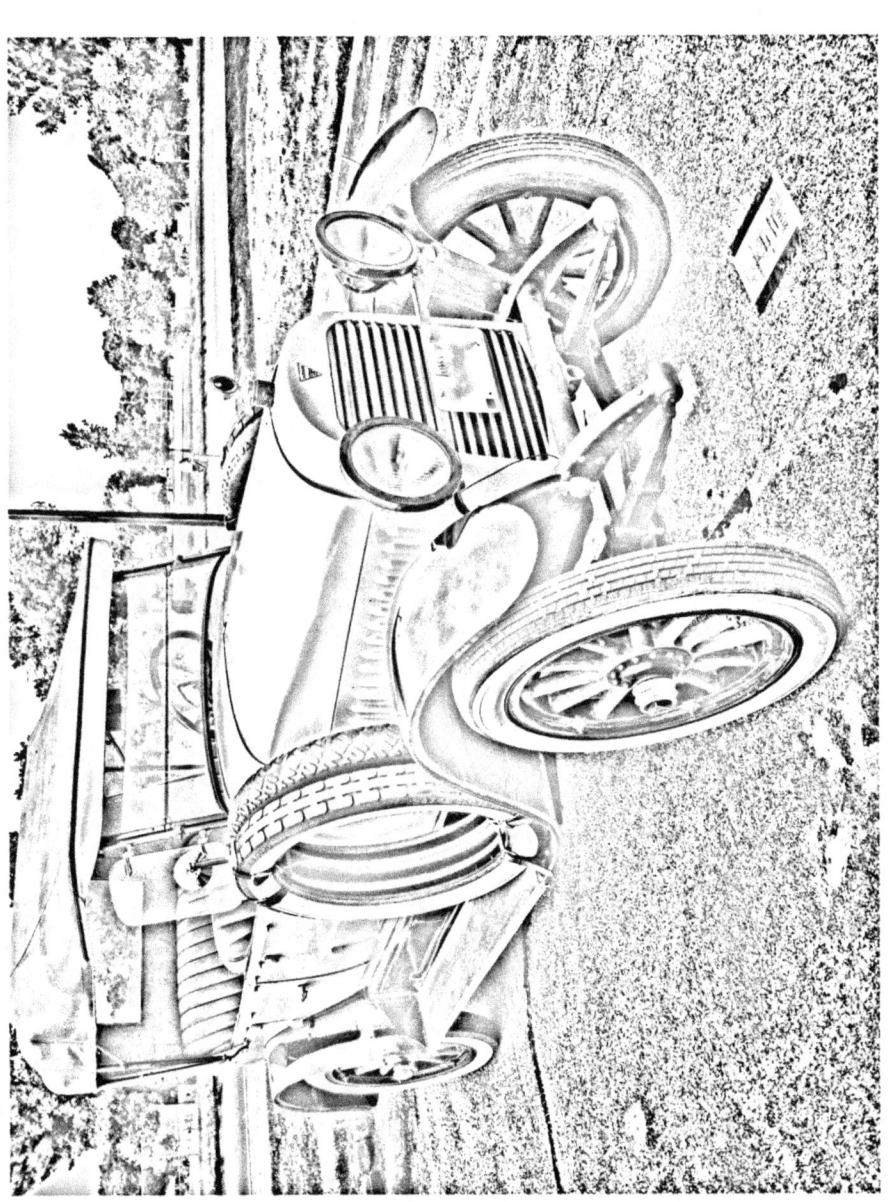

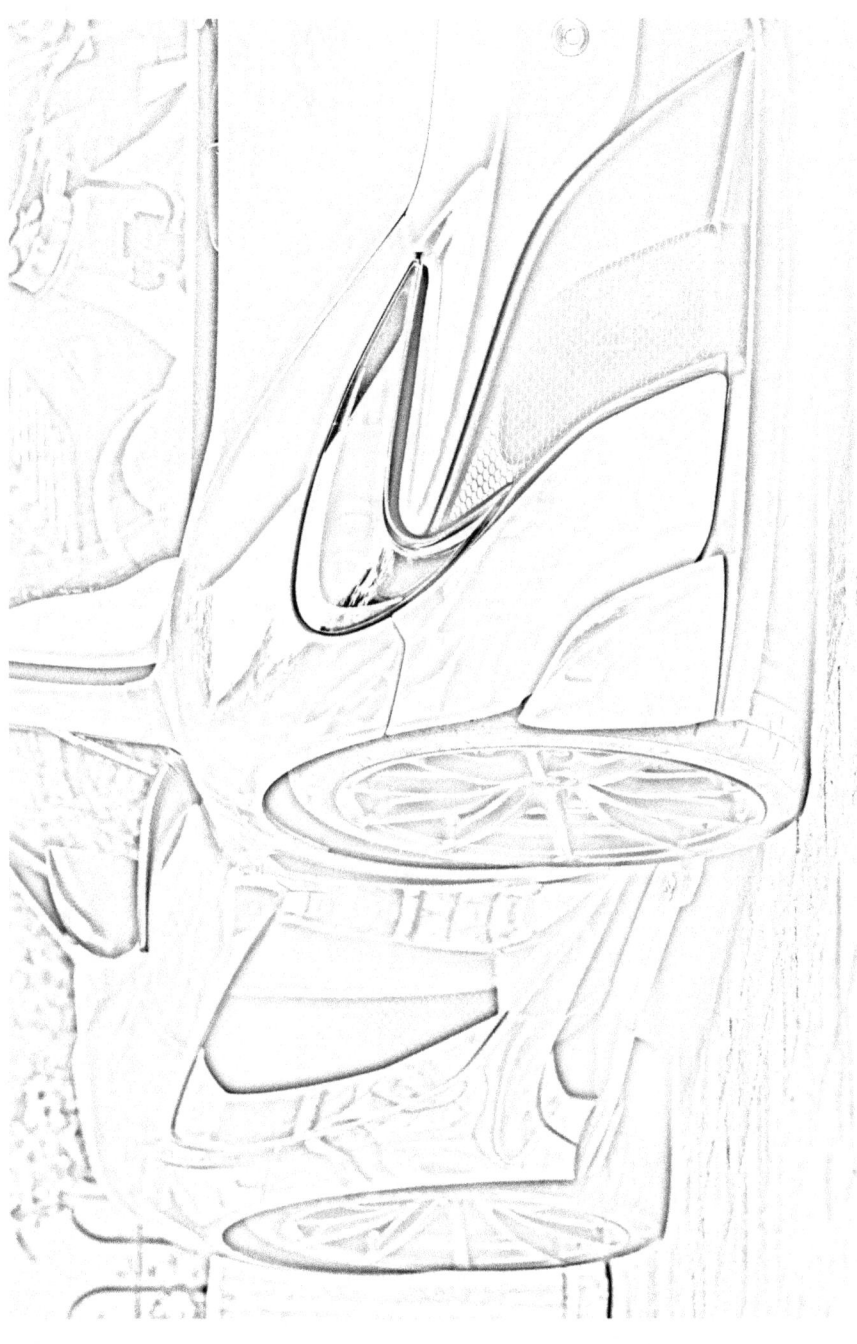

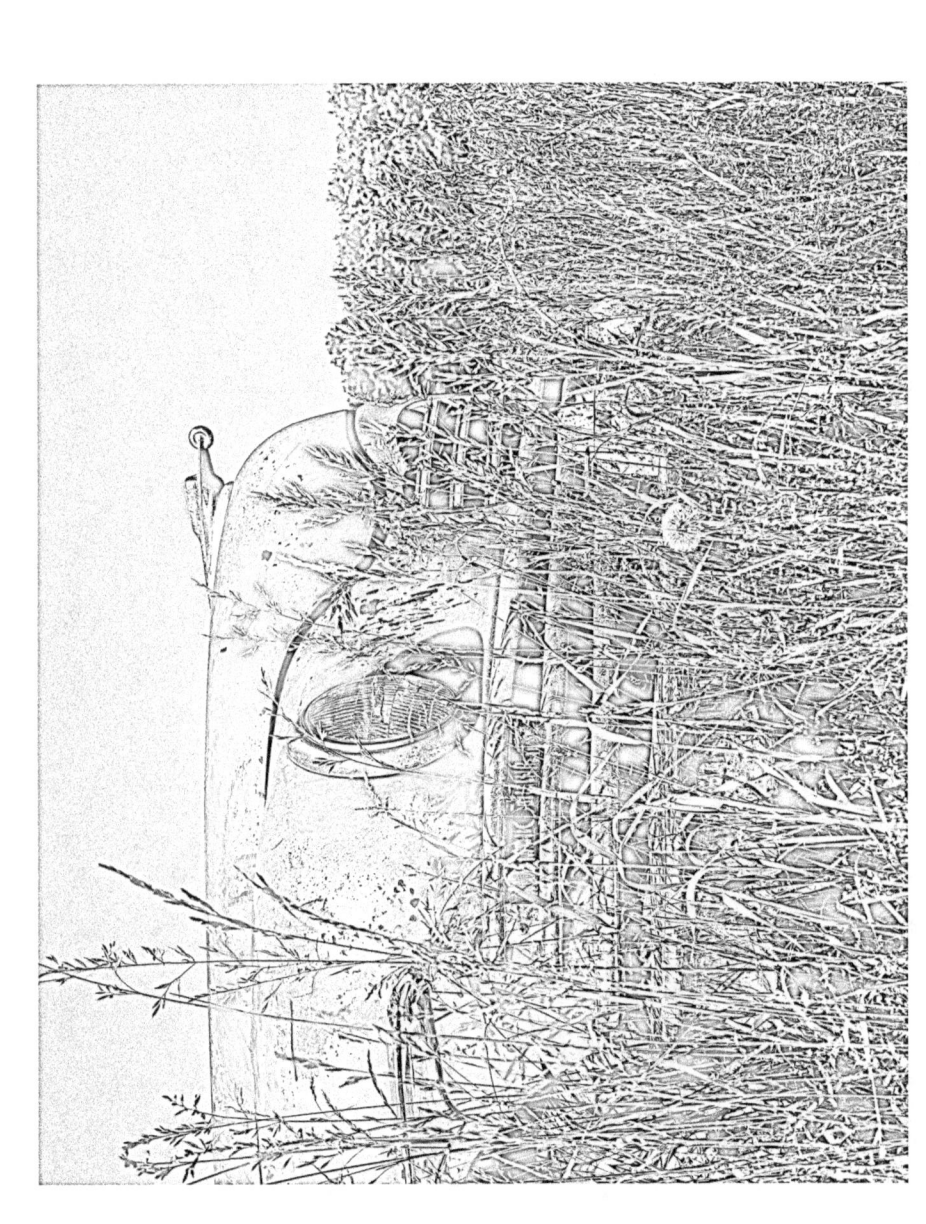

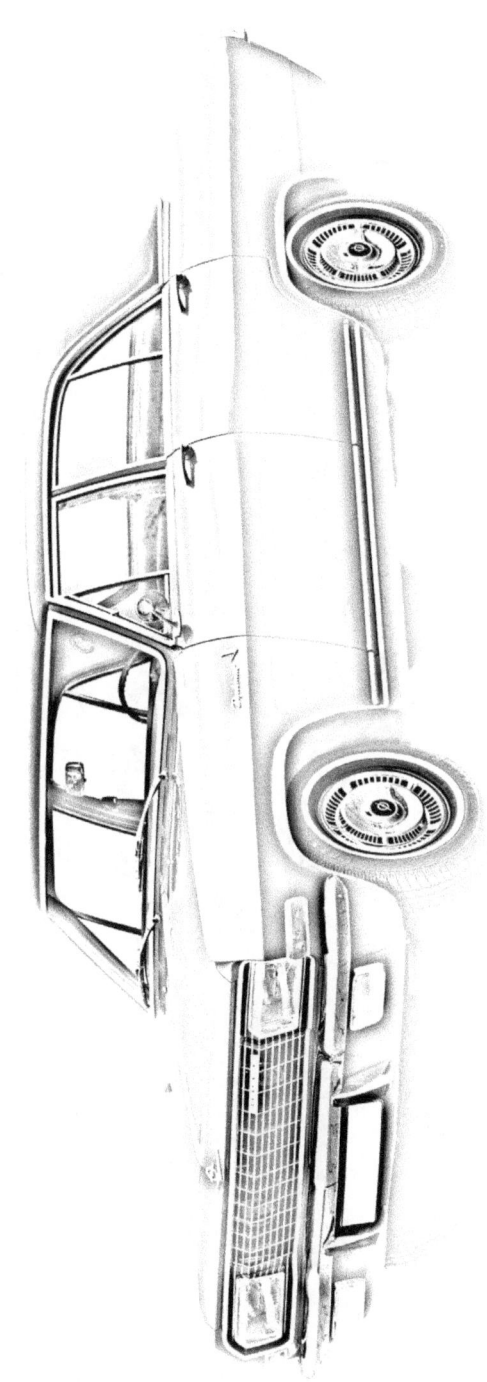

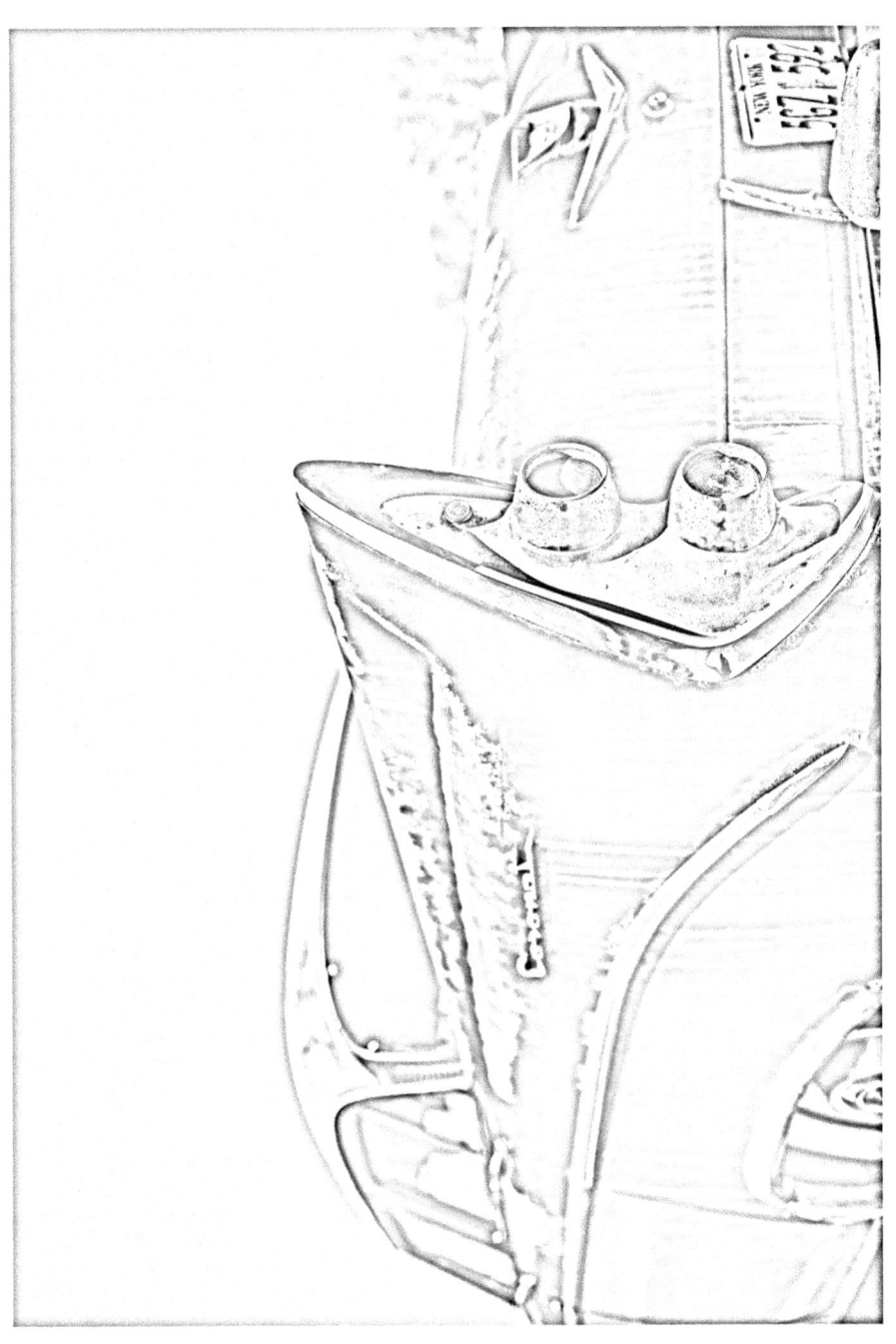

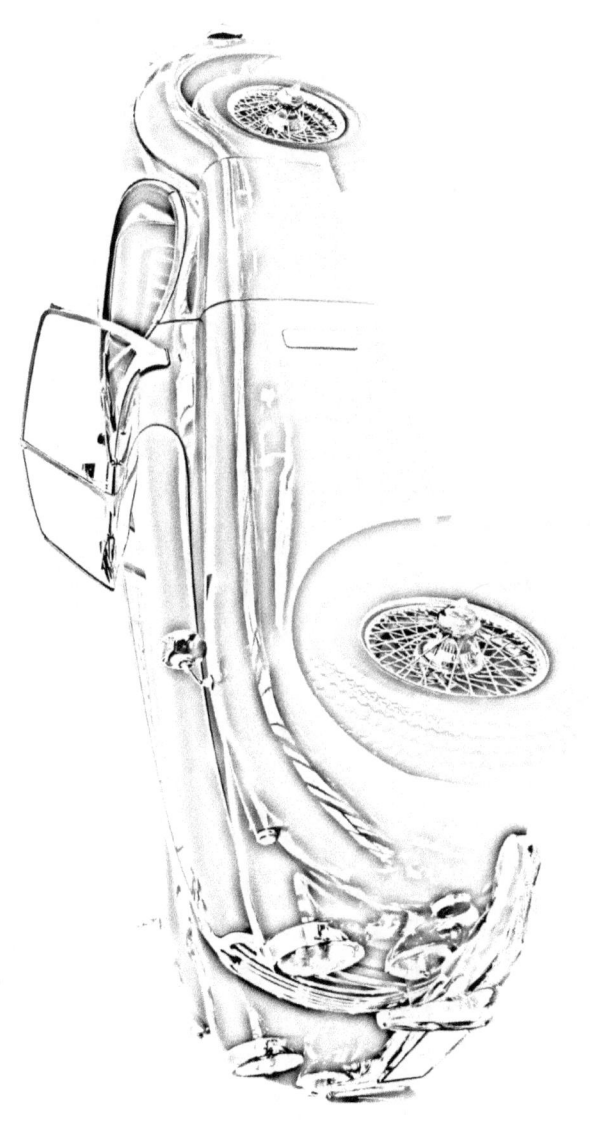

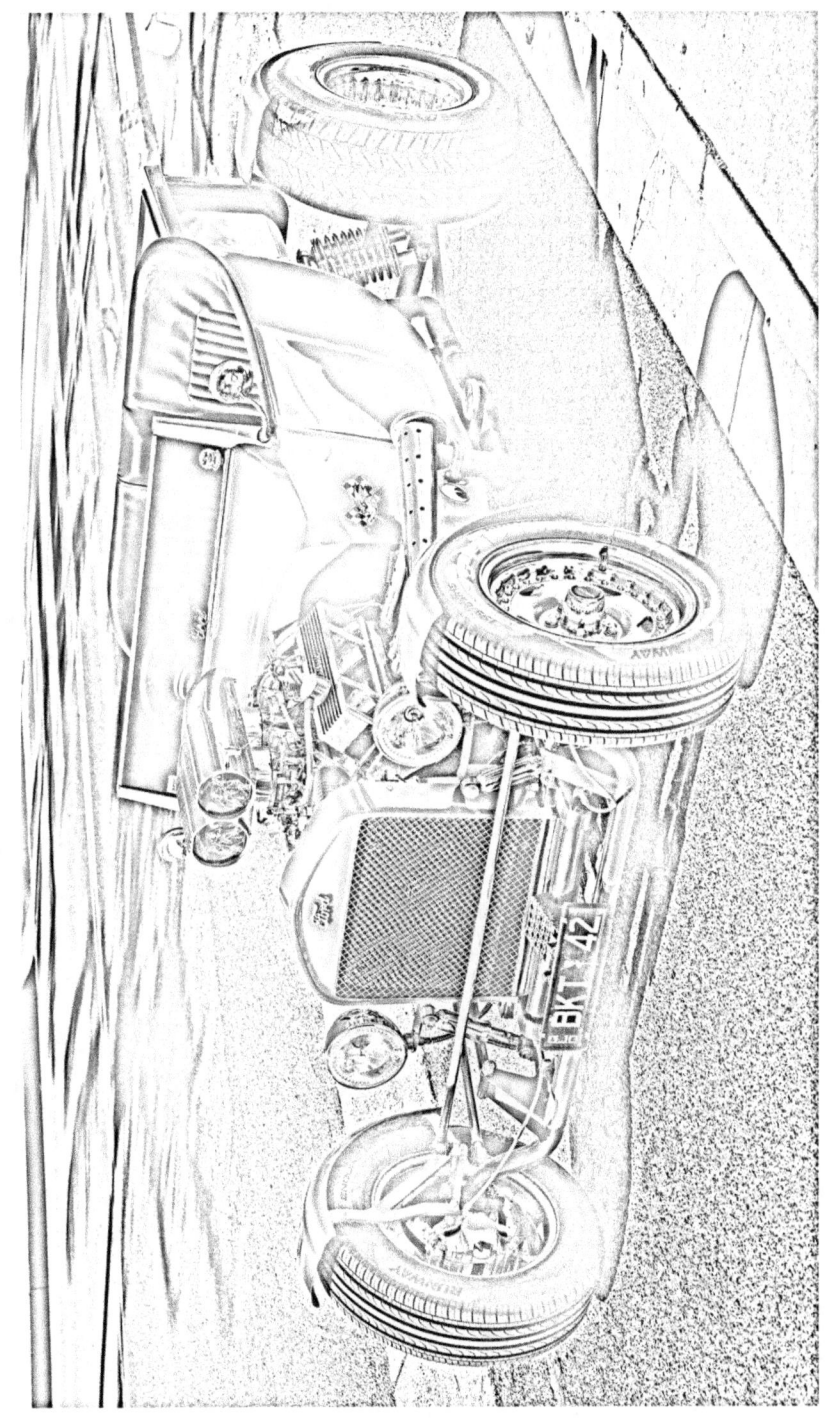

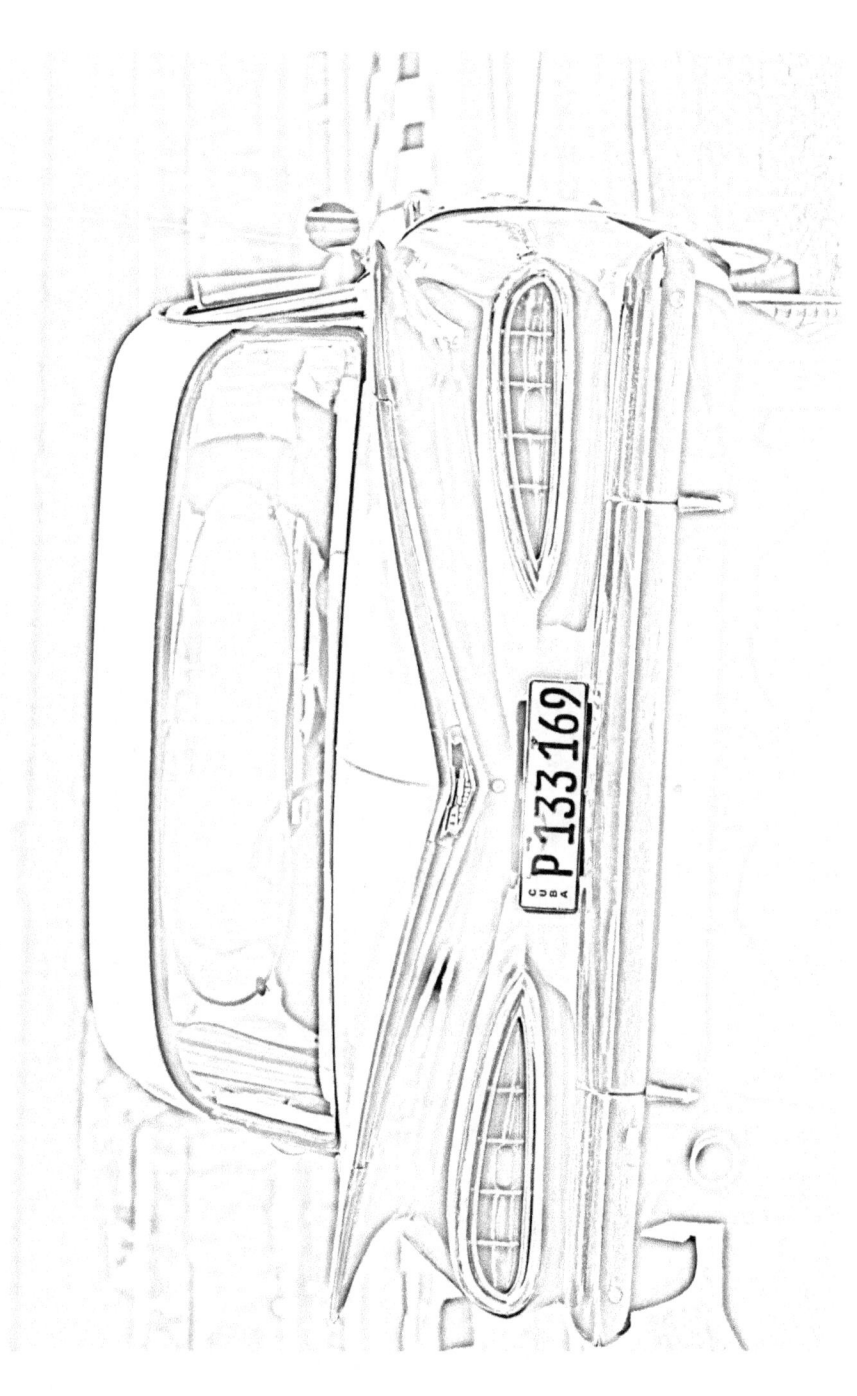

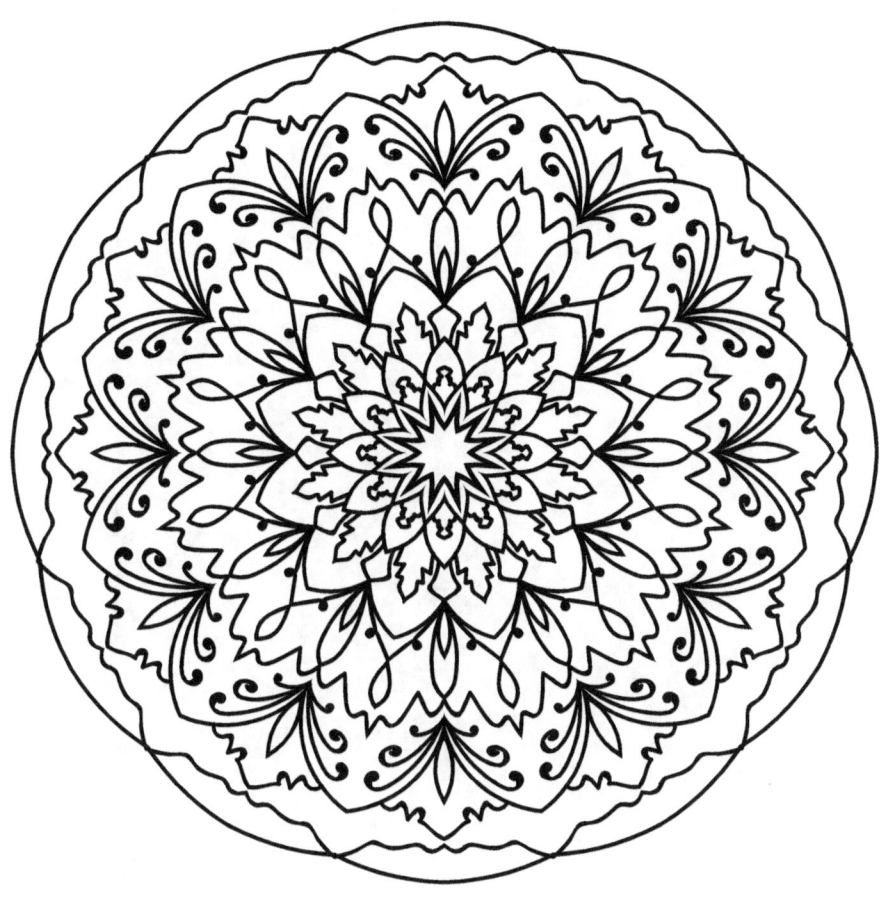

Look for other types of beautiful designs to color by author/illustrator Patricia Markham

(Mandala designs are featured in The Commuting Colorist Series - Books 1-5)

www.ingramcontent.com/pod-product-compliance
Lightning Source LLC
Chambersburg PA
CBHW070952220526
45471CB00007B/2998